TRAILBLAZING TEAMS

GROUPS OF PEOPLE WHO HAVE CHANGED THE WORLD

FIRST MEN

ON THE

MOON

WRITTEN BY

EMILIE DUFRESNE

DESIGNED BY

DANIELLE RIPPENGILL

BookLife PUBLISHING

©2021
BookLife Publishing Ltd.
King's Lynn
Norfolk PE30 4LS

ISBN: 978-1-83927-358-2

Written by:
Emilie Dufresne

Edited by:
Madeline Tyler

Designed by:
Danielle Rippengill

All facts, statistics, web addresses and URLs in this book were verified as valid and accurate at time of writing. No responsibility for any changes to external websites or references can be accepted by either the author or publisher.

USA

CONTENTS

Words that look like this can be found in the glossary on page 24.

MICHAEL COLLINS

To go places and do things that have never been done before - that's what living is all about.

Who is Michael Collins?

What part did he play on the Apollo 11 space flight?

COLLINS

BUZZ ALDRIN

Who is Buzz Aldrin?

How did he become
an astronaut?

I know the
sky is not the limit,
because there are
footprints on the
Moon - and I made
some of them!

NASA   ALDRIN

NEIL ARMSTRONG

That's one small step for a man, one giant leap for mankind.

Who was Neil Armstrong?

What did he do on the Moon?

THE MEN BEFORE THE MOON

MICHAEL COLLINS

Michael Collins was born in Italy in 1930.

He followed in his family's footsteps and joined the **military**. He then joined the US **air force** and became a pilot. He became part of **NASA**'s space programme in 1963.

MICHAEL COLLINS

BUZZ ALDRIN

Edwin Aldrin Jr, later Buzz Aldrin, was born in the US in 1930.

He too joined the US air force. Here he became a pilot before going to **university** to get a **PhD**, where he studied spacecraft.

BUZZ ALDRIN

NEIL ARMSTRONG

Neil Armstrong was born in 1930 in the US.

He earned his pilot's <u>licence</u> at 16. While at university, he trained as a pilot in the US <u>Navy</u>. He joined the <u>organisation</u> that would become NASA and worked as an <u>engineer</u> and pilot.

NEIL ARMSTRONG

A RACE TO THE STARS

In the mid-1950s, a race began between the US and the **Soviet Union**. The race was to the stars and both countries wanted to show that they had the best space technology.

The world's first human-made satellite, Sputnik 1, was launched by the Soviet Union in 1957.

The US spacecraft Apollo 11 was the first spacecraft to take people to the Moon.

Both countries wanted to be the first to launch satellites into **orbit** and put humans into space. One of the biggest goals they both shared was landing people on the Moon.

TRAILBLAZERS IN TRAINING

THEY LEARNED HOW TO TAKE ROCK SAMPLES.

THEY HAD TO PRACTISE DOING THEIR TASKS IN THEIR SPACESUITS.

Michael, Buzz and Neil went through a lot of training to be able to fly Apollo 11, land on the Moon, and collect samples from it. This is how the first men on the Moon trained for their mission.

BLAST OFF!

On July 16th, 1969, the Apollo 11 spacecraft launched from Earth. It travelled into Earth's orbit before making the journey into the Moon's orbit.

It is thought that over 600 million people watched the event on television.

Michael Collins stayed on his own in the spacecraft for a whole day while Buzz and Neil went down in the lunar module to carry out the tasks.

LUNAR MODULE

It was Michael's job to keep in contact with the scientists on Earth and make sure his teammates could get back to the spacecraft.

They took samples, planted an American flag, spoke to the US president and recorded it for the world to see.

Neil Armstrong was the first man to walk on the Moon, closely followed by Buzz Aldrin.

BUZZ ALDRIN'S FOOTPRINT

16

NASA   ARMSTRONG

A plaque is a flat piece of metal, often with words written on it, which celebrates a special occasion.

HERE MEN FROM THE PLANET EARTH
FIRST SET FOOT UPON THE MOON
JULY 1969, A. D.
WE CAME IN PEACE FOR ALL MANKIND

NEIL A. ARMSTRONG
ASTRONAUT

MICHAEL COLLINS
ASTRONAUT

EDWIN E. ALDRIN, JR.
ASTRONAUT

RICHARD NIXON
PRESIDENT, UNITED STATES OF AMERICA

The astronauts also left a plaque on the Moon, and a disc with recordings on it from over 70 countries. The messages show how Earth comes in peace.

17

DOWN TO EARTH

Neil and Buzz successfully re-joined Michael in the spacecraft.

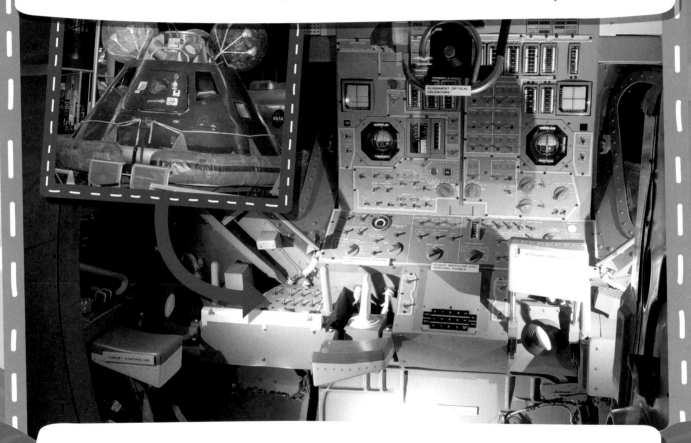

They began to make the journey back to Earth. They were cramped into the spacecraft with their equipment and they had a tough journey ahead of them.

There were storms on the part of the ocean where the astronauts were meant to land, so they had to quickly change direction and land in a safe part of the ocean.

12s

10e ANNIVERSAIRE DE L'HOMME SUR LA LUNE (1969 - 1979)

REPUBLIQUE DE GUINEE

Without all three of the team working together, the mission would not have been successful.

LEAVING A LEGACY

The successful Apollo 11 mission paved the way for space exploration and helped us to understand more about what the Moon was made of and how it came to be.

The rock samples collected on the mission are still used by scientists today.

NASA ALDRIN

The mission also became one of the most important moments in human history. It showed that we can do amazing things and take ourselves to amazing places – even the Moon.

A TRAILBLAZING TIMELINE

1957

SPUTNIK I IS PUT INTO ORBIT

1930

MICHAEL, BUZZ AND NEIL ARE BORN

1955

NEIL ARMSTRONG JOINS WHAT WOULD LATER BECOME NASA

1950s

THE SPACE RACE BEGINS

NASA

LLINS

2012

NEIL ARMSTRONG DIES

1963

MICHAEL COLLINS AND BUZZ ALDRIN JOIN NASA

NASA

1969

APOLLO 11 MAKES A SUCCESSFUL MISSION TO THE MOON

ARMSTRONG

GLOSSARY

air force	a part of the armed forces to do with aeroplanes and flying
engineer	a person who designs and builds machines
licence	a document that allows someone to use something, such as drive a car or fly a plane
military	being in or relating to the armed forces
NASA	National Aeronautics and Space Administration, the space agency in the US
navy	a part of the armed forces to do with the boats and the sea
orbit	the curved path an object takes around another, often larger, object in space
organisation	a group of people who work together to achieve certain things
PhD	a type of degree given to people who have done a lot of research into a particular subject
samples	small parts of something which are taken and then tested by scientists
satellite	a human-made object that is put into the orbit of a planet or moon
Soviet Union	a country that used to exist and eventually split up to make the countries of Russia, Ukraine and others
university	a place where people go to study, usually after they are 18

INDEX

24